mck

A New True Book

THE AZTEC

By Patricia McKissack

CHILDRENS PRESS™

CHICAGO

Pyramid of the Sun

PHOTO CREDITS

©Reinhard Brucker—8 (bottom right), 19

Image Finders:
©A. Data—17 (left)

Historical Pictures Service, Inc., Chicago—
4, 7, 14 (right), 43

Nawrocki Stock Photo:
  ©D.J. Variakojis—2, 8 (top right), 10,
17 (right), 28, 44 (right)
  ©Jim Whitmer—12 (right)
  ©Jeff Apoian—45 (center and right)

Odyssey Productions, Chicago—Cover,
8 (left: top and bottom), 12 (left), 14 (left),
15, 16, 21, 22, 24, 26, 27, 30, 33 (2 photos),
34, 35, 36, 37, 38, 40, 44 (left)

Peabody Museum, Harvard University—45
(left)

Cover: Diego Rivera mural of Tenochtitlán,
  ancient Aztec capital

Library of Congress Cataloging in Publication Data

McKissack, Pat, 1944-
  The Aztec.

  (A New true book)
  Includes index.
  Summary: Discusses the Aztec, their history,
religion, language, customs, and final days.
  1. Aztec—Juvenile literature. [1. Aztec 2. Indians of
Mexico] I. Title.
F1219.73.M38 1985   972'.01   84-23142
ISBN 0-516-01936-8   AACR2

TABLE OF CONTENTS

Hernando Cortés kneels before Montezuma, the Aztec king.

SPAIN COMES TO MEXICO

The Aztec believed
that one of their spirits
had white skin and a
beard. This spirit sailed
away on a raft made of
snakes but promised to
return. In 1519, Montezuma II,
king of the Aztec, was told
that white-skinned, bearded
men were coming.
Montezuma believed the
Aztec spirit had returned.

At first the strangers
were welcomed. Soon,

however, Montezuma learned that their leader, Hernando Cortés, was not an Aztec spirit. Cortés and his men had come to conquer the New World for the king of Spain.

The Aztec greatly outnumbered the 503 Spanish soldiers. But their bows and arrows were no match for Spanish cannons and crossbows. After many battles, the Aztec were

An early Aztec drawing shows the power of the Spanish soldiers.

defeated on August 13, 1521.

Who were these people the Spaniards called the Aztec?

Objects found in or near Mexico City—a stone head, two stone structures, a piece of pottery—give clues to the Aztec way of life.

THE RISE OF THE AZTEC

What we know about the Aztec comes from three sources: Aztec "picture books," diaries and records kept by the Spaniards, and objects found by archaeologists.

Humans lived in Mexico as early as 11,000 B.C. People wandered from north to south looking for food. By 6500 B.C. many Native Americans had settled in Mexico. Some

A carved boulder at La Venta stands as a reminder of Olmec art.

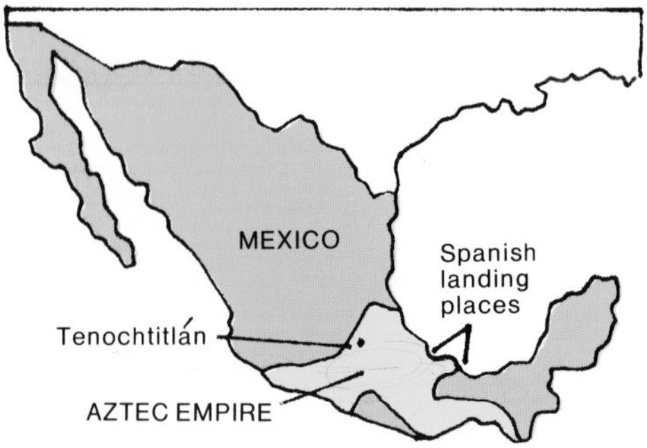
MEXICO
Spanish landing places
Tenochtitlán
AZTEC EMPIRE

of the early people of Mexico were the Olmec, the Zapotec, the Maya, the Toltec, the Mixtec, and the Chichimec. Most were farmers. Their main crop was maize (corn).

About A.D. 1200 the
Tenocha people moved
into the Valley of Mexico.
After many battles with
their neighbors, they
settled on an island in the
middle of Lake Texcoco—
"The Lake of the Moon."
From this island they built
the powerful nation the
Spaniards called the Aztec.

Aztec history records it
differently.

The image of the eagle and the snake that guided the Aztec to a new land today appears on the flag of Mexico and important buildings.

The Aztec had a story of how they came to the Valley of Mexico. Huitzilopochtli, or Left-Handed Hummingbird, the main spirit of the Aztec, told the people to

stop wandering when they
saw an eagle holding a
snake while sitting on a
prickly pear cactus on a
swampy island. They
reportedly saw this sight
on an island in Lake
Texcoco. And that is where
they settled.

The early Aztec people
built a temple dedicated to
Left-Handed Hummingbird
and to the rain spirit, Tlaloc.
They added to this temple
several times.

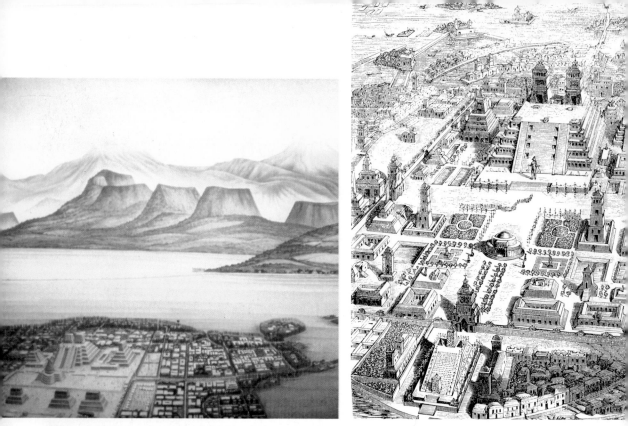

Many artists try to show how the great capital of Tenochtitlán (tay • NAWCH • tee • TLAHN), a city of over 100,000 people, would have looked during the Aztec empire.

The Aztec capital was Tenochtitlán. The city was rich with gold, silver, and rare jewels. The great temple and the king's

A scale model of Tenochtitlán has been made at the Museum of Anthropology in Mexico City.

palace were splendid buildings.

The Aztec nation lasted from 1325 to 1521. The kings ruled many thousands of people from Tenochtitlán.

RELIGION

Although they had many different spirits, the Aztec mainly worshiped the sun spirit. Aztec priests offered human sacrifices to keep the sun spirit happy.

There were hundreds of priests and priestesses.

A sun altar of enemy skulls was placed near every Aztec temple. The Aztec believed the sun fought darkness every night, but rose each morning to save mankind.

Two of the many spirits that were part of Aztec religious beliefs

They led hundreds of rituals. They predicted the future and acted as doctors. They also taught counting, writing, science, history, art, music, and dance.

LANGUAGE, COUNTING, AND CALENDAR

The Aztec language
is called Nahuatl. Like
the ancient Egyptians,
the Aztec used pictures
to write their language.
The pictures were
used to represent words.
For example, a picture of
a foot meant travel. The
Aztec wrote about their
history, their religion,

Aztec picture writing recorded history and business and religious information.

and daily life. They also
wrote poetry. Unfortunately,
the Spaniards destroyed
many of their books.
Today, only a few remain
in museums.

The Aztec had a counting system. Dots represented numbers from 1 to 19. A flag was number 20, a feather was 400, and a bag was 8,000.

The Aztec people had a 360-day calendar. It had eighteen parts with twenty days each. The five extra days were called "empty days." On those days all work stopped. No fires were made. The people

The Great Calendar Stone showed the days of the Aztec year.
It also foretold solar eclipses and a great earthquake.

fasted. At the end of the
five days, the Aztec priests
made a human sacrifice;
new fires were lit. Life and
the calendar began again.

This famous mural by Diego Rivera shows how three classes of Aztec people lived.

THE PEOPLE

The Aztec had three social classes: the nobility, the merchants and craftsmen, and the peasants.

The Aztec had slaves who could buy or earn their freedom. The children of slaves were born free.

Most of the people were farmers who lived in family units. These units were parts of larger groups called *calpulli*, or clans.

Detail by Diego Rivera shows clan members building Tenochtitlán.

Each clan had its own leaders, judges, local priests, and schools. Land was owned by the clan.

A clan member was expected to serve in the army or work on building projects. Men who proved themselves in war, excelled in a craft, or served the government well could rise in the social order. Talented girls could become wives of the noble class.

Peasant women made family clothing using a coarse, colorless cloth made from the agave plant. Peasant men wore a white cloak, called a *tilmantli*, tied over the right shoulder.

A scale model of the Aztec market place is on exhibit
at the Museum of Anthropology in Mexico City.

Peasant women dressed
in ankle-length skirts and
blouses. Sandals were
worn only on special
occasions.

Merchants, craftsmen,
and the nobility tied their
tilmantli under their chins.

Diego Rivera mural showing Aztec headdresses

They also decorated their clothing. Upper-class men and women wore fine jewelry, feathered headdresses, and sandals made from jaguar skins.

Aztec priests wore black hooded cloaks.

The birth of a baby was a joyful occasion. Clan members brought gifts. Girls were named after something pretty, such as flowers or birds. Boys were given powerful names taken from nature.

Young dancers perform the traditional dances of their ancestors at the Fiesta San Miguel, San Miguel de Allende, Mexico.

Each clan had two schools called "Houses of Youth"—one for boys and one for girls. Children began school at age three.

The schools were strict. Boys learned citizenship, religion, dance, music, crafts, history, and warfare. They stayed in school until they married and began farming. If they showed promise, they were sent to the capital to study under

Today, people enjoy seeing the Ballet Folklorico of Mexico perform ancient Aztec dances.

the high priests. Ordinarily this was the privilege of the noble class.

Girls were taught crafts, songs, music, art, healing arts, dance, and history. Often they, too, were sent to school in the capital.

Boys usually married at age twenty, girls at sixteen. The parents made all the arrangements. A priest studied the "signs" to see if the marriage would be a good one.

The marriage ceremony was simple. The bride and groom tied their shirttails together. This "tying of the knot" was supposed to bind the couple together for life. Commoners had only one wife; nobles could have more.

EVERYDAY LIFE

Peasant houses were made of reeds and mud. Inside, the one-room, windowless house was divided in two—the kitchen and the sleeping area.

Houses of the wealthy were larger and made of dried brick called adobe.

The Aztec ate corn cakes, beans, sweet potatoes, avocados, squash,

Nobles, slaves, soldiers, farmers, and traders crowded the busy Aztec markets.

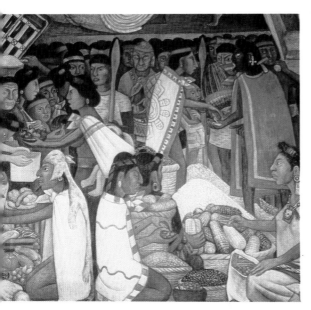

peppers (chilis), fish, fowl, deer, turkey, and dog. They also ate popcorn!

Aztec peasants grew most of their food. They traded for other things in marketplaces.

Men and boys hunted with blowguns, spears, clubs, and rocks.

Everybody worked from dawn until dusk. Work was done without the help of animals. Although the Aztec knew about the wheel, they didn't use it.

The Aztec worked without the help of animals.

Statue of an ancient Aztec spirit, Tlaloc, stands
outside the Museum of Anthropology.

Like everything else in
Aztec life, their sports and
games were connected to
religious festivals. The
most popular sport was
like basketball. Children
played board games, hide-
and-seek, running games,
and tag.

An Aztec temple
vase being restored

MERCHANTS, CRAFTSMEN, AND NOBILITY

Merchants traveled to
far-off places to bring back
goods the people needed,
such as cotton, cacao,
rubber, jade, pottery,

Montezuma's headdress

feathers, nuts, herbs, and medicines. They sold fun items, too. Chicle, for example, was very popular. From chicle the Aztec made chewing gum.

Aztec craftsmen made jewelry, pottery, metalwork, and feathered headdresses. Many served the king as architects and engineers.

A mural by Diego Rivera shows Aztec nobility.

Aztec nobility was the ruling class. Among them were local clan leaders, district leaders, judges, public officials, tax collectors, military captains, record keepers, priests, and advisers to the king.

ARTS AND SCIENCES

Aztec dancing, singing, music, and poetry were part of all religious festivals.

The Aztec made music with flutes, drums, whistles, and rattles. Often during a ceremony the priests would chant this poem:

. . . Here we come to meet;
We are only passersby on earth.

Aztec artists sculpted in stone, rock, crystal, turquoise, and jade. They painted murals on indoor

and outdoor walls. They worked in clay, gold, and silver. Religious subjects were Aztec themes. Their love of nature also was shown in all their art.

The Aztec used herbs and roots to heal.

THE ONE WHO SPEAKS

The Aztec kings were "elected" for life by a council of high officials. The king was head of both Aztec religion and Aztec government. "The One Who Speaks" was the king's official title, because he spoke for all Aztec people.

The king listened to his advisers. He took tribute (taxes) from conquered nations. He approved or rejected building projects.

THE FINAL DAYS

Montezuma II had ruled for sixteen years when Hernando Cortés landed.

Montezuma's priests reported bad signs in the heavens. To the priests these signs meant doom. When Montezuma heard that white men were coming, he sent gifts of gold and silver, hoping they would take the gifts and go away. But once the Spaniards saw the riches,

Montezuma was killed on June 30, 1520.

nothing could turn them back. They were determined to see more. And the rest is history.

The Spaniards destroyed the capital and took most of its wealth back to Spain. Montezuma was killed. The Aztec became Spanish subjects.

Left: Archaeologists have found Aztec ruins
in the Zócalo area of Mexico City.
Above: Aztec serpent sculpture.

Three hundred years
after Spain conquered
Mexico, the new Mexican
people fought for, and won,
their independence.

Today, Lake Texcoco has
dried up; the great Temple
of the Sun is buried under
modern Mexico City.

44

　　But there are still Aztec
people living in Mexico.
They still speak Nahuatl,
the language of their
ancestors, and they continue
to make outstanding
contributions to the arts,
sciences, and culture of
Mexico and the world.

WORDS YOU SHOULD KNOW

ancestors(AN • sess • terz) — early family members, usually those who have been dead for many years

archaeologists(ar • kee • AHL • uh • jists) — people who study very old objects, buildings, ruins, etc., to learn about the ancient people who used them

clan(KLAN) — a group of related families

cloak(KLOHK) — a loose piece of clothing, often reaching the floor, and usually fastened at the neck or shoulders

conquer(KONG • ker) — to win or defeat, usually by the use of weapons

council(KOWN • sil) — a group of people, usually elected or appointed, that gives official advice, chooses leaders, passes laws, etc.

craftsmen(KRAFTS • men) — people who create things by hand, especially useful and beautiful things

crossbow(KROSS • boh) — an arrow-shooting weapon that has a bow fastened crosswise to a long wooden stick

human sacrifice(HYOO • min SACK • ruh • fice) — the killing of a human in a religious ceremony, often to show respect or fear toward some spirit

merchants(MUR • chents) — people who buy, sell, or trade

nobility(no • BIL • it • ee) — the upper or ruling class in certain countries

peasants(PEZ • ents) — people of lower class, often uneducated, who farm or work for the upper class

ritual(RICH • oo • il) — a ceremony acted out by following certain social or religious rules

temple(TEM • puhl) — a building in which religious ceremonies are held

tribute(TRIB • yoot) — the payment of money or valuables by a conquered nation to the government of the conquering nation

INDEX

About the author

Patricia C. McKissack and her husband, Fredrick, are freelance writers, editors, and teachers of writing. They are the owners and operators of All-Writing Services, located in Clayton, Missouri. Ms. McKissack, an award-winning editor, published author, and experienced educator, has taught writing at several St. Louis colleges and universities, including Lindenwood College, the University of Missouri at St. Louis, and Forest Park Community College.

Since 1975, Ms. McKissack has published numerous magazine articles and stories for juvenile and adult readers. She has also conducted educational and editorial workshops throughout the country for a number of organizations, businesses, and universities.

Patricia McKissack is the mother of three teenage sons. They all live in a large remodeled inner-city home in St. Louis. Aside from writing, which she considers a hobby as well as a career, Ms. McKissack likes to take care of her many plants.